Polish Your Appearance
The Modern Gentleman's Guide for Style and Image

BY ALEXANDER PEZO
Volume 1

Copyright © 2019 By Alexander Pezo
All rights reserved

No part of this publication may be reproduced, stored in a retrieval system or transmitted in any way by means, electronic, mechanical, photocopy, recording or otherwise without the prior permission of the author except as provided by USA copyright law. The opinions expressed by the author are not necessarily those Alexander Pezo, LLC

Published by Alexander Pezo, LLC
www.alexanderpezo.com
Cover Art: Elam Entertainment & Productions
ISBN-13: 9781734614008

Table of Contents

CHAPTER 1	4
RED POLISH	4
CHAPTER 2	10
BET ON YOURSELF	10
CHAPTER 3	17
CREATING YOUR STYLE	17
CHAPTER 4	34
THE POLISHED MENTOR	34
CHAPTER 5	40
POLISH YOUR GROOMING	40
CHAPTER 6	46
ARROGANT & CONFIDENT APPEARANCE	46
ABOUT THE AUTHOR	54

INTRODUCTION

After spending 25 years in Senior Management for multiple Fortune 500 Companies as well as currently being the Regional Operations Manager for the world's largest day labor provider, I was thirsting to reflect and share with aspiring business professionals.

With that said, as my experiences allowed me to work with young males, several things had become blatantly apparent. The systemic mindset, which ultimately shapes us, starts at a very young age. Here is what I mean by this.

If your parents are on the system or public assistance, unless you are exposed to other situations that is all you will know. If you are a foster kid or have an (I.E.P.) **Individualized Educational Plan,** which helps students with learning disabilities and other challenges succeed in school, keep in mind it may help you for that time. However; your entire history with the program is tracked and documented.

Knowing that these obstacles will continue to perpetuate and exist, I set a goal to get as many young men that may not have a male influence in their life to understand the importance of *self-care*. Self-care is the *practice of taking an active role in protecting one's own well-being and happiness, during periods of stress.*

The reason why I stress this as a point of emphasis is that a great deal of males struggle outside their parents' nest with maintaining their self-care. I am so thankful for my Mom nurturing and teaching me the way that she did. I will delve into this more in Chapter 1, "**Red Polish**."

Creating the "Polish Your Appearance" platform while developing my skill-set as a designer that values presentation,

Alexander Pezo

I asked myself what are the key and vital measures that young professionals must consider when it pertains to their appearance?"

From a rhetorical perspective, this provoked a great deal of thought and opportunity to put together a *"How To"* book series. The first thing I said to myself is to write the book successfully, I could not find fault in what people may not know.

In the words of Albert Einstein, *"We cannot solve our problems with the same thinking we used when we created them."*

Plain and simple, in my own words, it's like this: *"Often times people are afraid to learn what they don't already know."*

With that being said, I spent the next year simply observing how individuals would dress to apply for work and come in for interviews. I capped the number of observations at 200.

In observing 200 applicants, only three came in with a resume, dress pants or khakis, and a button-down shirt. These numbers were so staggering and low that immediately it made me think of the Five P's *"Perfect Practice Prevents, Poor Performance."* Here is what this quote means.

As opposed to simply getting ready for a job, not only be ready for it, but dress and prepare everyday for the career that you desire.

I heard one of my three all-time favorite Pro Basketball Players Earvin "Magic" Johnson said in his Uninterrupted Kneading Dough interview with Maverick Carter,

Alexander Pezo

"I used to clean buildings for two black entrepreneurs from Friday to Sunday in East Lansing. I would get to the 7th-floor office and act as if I were the CEO. I would call and have my "assistant" Alisa to bring me coffee and donuts. I was only 16 at the time." In case you are wondering, Magic's reported net worth is over 500 million dollars.

Hearing Magic talk about how his desire to be successful at such an early age, made me think about my goals and drive for success as a kid. However; as a father of two beautiful daughters, Bria Kathleen and Milana Alexis, and son Jaxon Alexander, my mind immediately shifted to the sense of urgency I must continue to maneuver with to ensure their success. Paying it forward to my kids as well as positioning them for success is my version of Polishing My Appearance.

My Mom's version of "Polishing My Appearance" was busing me from the Northside of Cincinnati to the Eastside every day for a better quality of education. This is called priority-based education. There is a multitude of ways to "Polish Your Appearance" however; in volume one my primary focus is "betting on and investing in yourself."

CHAPTER 1

RED POLISH

I named the book "Polish Your Appearance" and more importantly, this chapter, "**Red Polish**," as it is unequivocally in part to my Mother, Yvonne Alexandria Mays, nicknamed "Red" due to the color of her hair.

Red had me just prior to her 16th birthday. Not long after I was born, my father enlisted in the Army hence leaving my Mom to be a single parent, but more importantly raising herself and a newborn at the same time. To be clear this is not a story about my shortcomings in life. However; it is more about how my mother, "Red" started the process of "Polishing My Appearance."

One summer, when I was just 8-years-old Red made a bold decision to bus me 45 minutes from the Northside of

Alexander Pezo

Cincinnati to the Eastside to attend Saint Francis De Sales for 3rd and 4th grade. Although I went on to St. Mark in the 5th grade, I eventually finished middle school, 6th-8th grade, at St. Cecilia's in a predominantly Caucasian area of Oakley. However; it was St. Francis De Sales that ultimately exposed me to kids from a variety of cultures other than African American.

The one year that I spent at St. Marks showed me that there were a great deal of African American families doing phenomenal things. My time at St. Cecilia's assisted with challenging me. For starters, I was the only Black kid in my class for three years. In addition to that, my grammar left something to be desired. Growing up in the inner-city just two blocks from the St. Ledger Projects meant survival was much more important than improving my speech. Little did I understand that improving my grammar, at the time, was just that – showing me how to survive the game of life.

With that said, my mother Red, placed me in this environment because as she would say; ***"Everyone wants to grow but growth is uncomfortable."*** In other words, she knew I would get ridiculed by some of the students at the school. She also knew this would force me to either "Polish My Appearance" in the areas I severely needed to or receive constant teasing.

To make things more challenging, I had to switch teams in baseball, which led me to play baseball for one of the most prominent and generationally wealthy families of Cincinnati in the Sweeney's. This team was made up of a hodgepodge of kids from all over the district.

This team was comprised of players from stable, middle-class two-parent households, primarily. Being exposed to this type of environment broadened my horizons and forced me to learn how to communicate differently. I was one of the poorest kids on the team, however I was very talented, which somewhat evened the playing field.

What really helped me through the transition were the three years that my Mom had invested in my Catholic School education and changing my environment. She knew my speech and dialect needed help because I had adjusted to speaking a certain way. For those reading this part, bear in mind, this does not mean an attempt to be someone you are not. Moreover, it means to work to improve yourself now so that it will not be as difficult later. Understand that you can be transplanted into a new environment and still maintain the core of your existence.

Looking back on the situation, Red was attempting to teach me *priority-based education*. *This means to pay for education now so that you can offset and avoid paying max high school or college tuition later*. This strategy is commonly used in suburban communities that utilize quality-free or private catholic education to put their kids in advantageous positions for the future. Somehow My Mom was able to struggle and put me through Catholic middle school from the 3rd through 8th grade.

The time and investment that she ultimately made in me, though tough at times, not only started the process towards "Polishing My Appearance," but taught me to communicate on another level. Having a solid base in anything is key and essential to growth. With that said, the impact that Red's decisions had on my life was paramount. Her guidance and direction were ahead of the curve at such a young age. In fact, for my freshman year, she sent me to one of the premier schools in Ohio: The Summit Country Day.

Alexander Pezo

To this date, The Summit Country Day School is second to none when it comes to producing students with high character, integrity and the moral fiber to excel amongst higher academia.

This was yet another opportunity that my Mom created for me to "Polish My Appearance" academically and athletically.

I took great advantage of what was placed in front of me athletically. As a Freshman I started Varsity basketball and made first team All-City and Honorable Mention All-State. However, academically, I struggled mightily! A great deal of those struggles came from me not taking advantage of the positions that "Red" had placed me in over the years. Looking back on the situation, I excelled academically when I was around a demographic that I related to. However, I struggled in grades 6-8 because I was the only Black in my classroom. It was a great deal of pressure placed on me for personal acceptance as opposed to academic achievement. This carried over into my freshman year of high school as well. I eventually graduated from Purcell Marian High School which received its claim to fame for alum such as Dallas Cowboy great, Roger Staubach and Golden State Warrior Derrick Dickey.

Alexander Pezo

I really lacked confidence in myself academically because at no point in my life had anyone ever built me up mentally when it came to this part of my appearance. As a father, this helped me truly understand and grasp the importance of teaching my daughters words such as CAN and not even acknowledging CAN'T. I recognize that positive reinforcement and encouraging the heart are just as vital to their maturation and growth as well. For my son I need to model the way.

I remember Red told me, *"Son I cannot afford anything outside of your education. However, I can put you in position to meet that kind of people."*

In a nutshell, she was saying in her own way, *Carpe Diem*. Translation: "Seize the day." The fundamental message that still resonates with me to this day is simple. It's that no matter how bad someone wants better for you; you must want it for yourself. So, after not being able to find my footing academically throughout high school, I decided that if you look good, you feel good.

I really struggled with my confidence and style until my Junior year. After getting my first job at Skyline Chili for the spring and summer of 87, I asked my Mom if I could start buying my own clothing. Growing up, as I searched to find and eventually create my own fashion identity, I soon figured out that style is less about what you wear and more about how you wear it.

Keep in mind that Polishing Your Appearance does not happen overnight. In fact, it will take a great deal of what I refer to as repeating the 5-P's and experiencing some failure to grow. Understanding that perfect, practice, prevents poor performance is your roadmap to consistency and success — the 5 P's. I will touch on this matter in a later chapter dedicated to arrogance versus confidence.

More importantly, I recognized the importance of self-awareness when it came to shaping and "Polishing My Appearance." I left out the fact that prior to receiving my birth name, I was given the "nickname" of P.J. This stands for "Pride & Joy."

So, after finishing college and getting into corporate America at the age of 23, I vowed to myself that I would accomplish whatever I set my mind to. To me, this meant becoming my best me.

CHAPTER 2

BET ON YOURSELF

One of my favorite quotes and or sayings I heard came from good friend and CEO, Ron Harris from East Orange, New Jersey. He says, *"Always be more substance than show."*

This means that in addition to looking the part, one must always carry themselves in a manner that sets them apart from their competition. I will delve into this later in the books final chapter of *"Arrogance versus Confidence."*

Remember, *"The individual should always make the suit (or outfit) and the suit (or outfit) should not make them."* Often on the exterior we look great, but we are broken on the inside. Understand our true appearance is shaped and formed from the inside out.

The great Aristotle once said, *"The aim of art is to represent not the outward appearance of things, but their inward significance."*

Polishing Your Appearance means someone that shows confidence and knows how to behave socially.

They are charming, articulate and an excellent negotiator. More importantly, they have very high standards.

Alexander Pezo

One might ask to explain the importance of having high standards. Well, it's simple. Your standards will ultimately decide your level of education, circle of friends, financial status, and potentially your quality of life.

The world's most renown speaker, Tony Robbins once said; *"Set high standards for yourself and don't settle for anything less. You are the best judge of yourself and your capabilities."*

Polishing Your Appearance is a state of mind that will lead you to an array of success in a multitude of arenas.

You must be willing to take mental ownership to enhance your growth and development. One of my favorite quotes by my first professional mentor, George Williams, was *"Plan the work and work the plan."* Keep in mind, statistics show that 90% of our plans are never committed to paper. Then we wonder why the plan is not yielding the type of success and results that we expect. So, we need to recognize exactly what it is that we are polishing so to speak.

What exactly does "betting on yourself mean?" *This means understanding the power of priority-based investing in oneself with a strategic end game and goal in mind.*

You can find some of these similarities with individuals such as Jay-Z and Emory Jones. Documents of how Jay-Z assisted with Emory Jones' release from prison are now circulating the web. Emory Jones, Jay-Z's close friend and cousin, was released from prison in 2010. Emory had been locked-up in January 2000, after pleading guilty to a cocaine trafficking charge and was sentenced to nearly 16 years in prison. Allegedly, Emory ran a coke ring in Maryland's Eastern Shore.

Jay-Z & Emory Jones best friends and business partner of Roc Nation and Puma always says; *"You have to bet on yourself."* Too often we misconstrue the difference between betting on ourselves with investing in others' dreams. We simply choose to consume instead of investing and have nothing to show for it until it is too late.

Consumer Vs Priority Based Investing

A *Consumer* is a *person who purchases goods and services for personal use*. The American culture is one that wastes a ton and consumes even more without having any ownership or building wealth in most cases. The difference with *Priority Based Investing* is *Superiority in position, rank, and privilege in which endows someone or something with a quality or attribute.*

To *Endow* means*, provide with a quality, ability, or asset that is beneficial.*

I walked into a room and asked everyone to cover their eyes with one hand and use the other to answer the following questions: How many of you own the latest iPhone or Android? How many of you own a high-end handbag or Jordan's?

Alexander Pezo

IPHONE

MICHAEL KORS

Now how many of you own at least three suits or blazer combinations for a first, second and final job interview? How many of you own a pair of brown, black and cordovan shoes with a matching belt?

Alexander Pezo

Black Capped Toe Shoe

Brown Shoe

Cordovan Split Toe

Alexander Pezo

How many of you own at least two crisp button-down shirts and three ties? These are all examples of **Priority Based Investing.** In both cases, purchasing the right attire as well as betting on yourself shows how important it is to have an invested interest as opposed to a consumer interest. Here are some of the looks that will catapult and give you the upper hand once you decided to bet on yourself.

After I speak with most groups of aspiring young professionals, this is normally where they reveal their lack of priority-based investing in themselves. In fact, this mindset is the opposite of what many successful and wealthy people will say.

Billionaire and entrepreneur, Warren Buffet says, *"The most important investment you can make is in yourself."* Buffett is worth a reported $84.4 billion.

The mindset of investing in yourself must start at home when you are young. As the father of a boy, I take pride in helping to shape and mold Jaxon with my wife.

Our goal is to instill as much confidence in him as possible so that he understands there are no limitations on his success. Also, we want to surround him with individuals that will force his growth.

Ernst Haeckel said, *"Nothing is constant but change! All existence is a perpetual flux of "being and becoming!" That is the broad lesson of the evolution of the world."*

Basically, Ernst is saying that you must adapt and adjust, but more importantly, you can "Polish Your Appearance" by not setting boundaries and limitations on yourself.

CHAPTER 3

CREATING YOUR STYLE

Knowing Your Color Palette

Now let's discuss what your color palette means. Your palette is simply toning and colors that compliment your skin tone. One of the biggest mistakes I see in fashion is simply putting the wrong colors or fit on a body type or skin tone.

However, once you discover the colors that best fit your complexion you can now build from there. I suggest you start with pants first.

For starters, it is mandatory that you have the following color pants: **grey, navy blue, black, tan and olive**. I would recommend that you purchase non-pleated pants so that the fit is more tampered, and they can be dressed up or down.

If you are searching, starting a new job, or simply in need of enhancing your wardrobe, always start with an earth-tone palette. *These tones are pure colors that include black, white, and all grays, while near-neutral hues include browns, tan and darker colors.* Many earth tones originate from clay earth pigments, such as umber, ochre, and Sienna. These tones allow you to mix and match as well as coordinate your wardrobe without appearing repetitive. At first glance, colors such as these may appear to be boring, dated and overly conservative. However; earth tones are rich, timeless and versatile.

A key factor in expanding your wardrobe is simply understanding your budget. For example, there are times when I walk through high-end department stores to do what I call "*Style shopping*." There is a big difference between *style shopping* and *window shopping*. Here is the difference between the two:

Style shopping is going into a store to find pieces that meet the criteria or look that you are going for. This provides you with the option to see, touch, and feel it. This will give you a better understanding as to how it is made along with the cut and fit.

Often, when I go into high-end stores I never purchase unless it is on sale or at a severely reduced price. In most cases I find another store that offers the same type of fabrication. However, it is not name brand. This normally reduces the price drastically and provides the opportunity to enhance my look on a budget while presenting a more polished appearance.

Window Shopping **is simply the activity of looking at the goods displayed in shop windows, without intending to buy anything.**

Looking at consignment shops, second-hand stores, the Good Will and clearance racks are normally great places to start.

Now that we have taken a moment to highlight some points of emphasis and provided you some pointers on where to look, let's create your wardrobe using the spoke and wheel model.

Alexander Pezo

The *Spoke and Wheel Model* is simply when you start with a centerpiece or pieces that are related to an additional piece in your wardrobe. For example, if you have a pair of pants as the hub, then the rest of the wheel should be filled with items that complement the pants such as shirts, belts, socks, and shoes.

I would strongly encourage and recommend that you find individuals whose style and creativity you respect. In fact, here are some Instagram pages that you can follow as a reference point. @alexanderpezobrand and @thewaltheguy.

Alexander Pezo

"Dress for the response you are looking to receive, not your circumstance"

Alexander Pezo

I once heard that *"Style is a reflection of your attitude and your personality."* In knowing this, always remember that when you look good, you feel good. The image that you project to others is how they will often receive you. The great Snoop Dogg once said; *"You do not get a second chance to make a first impression."*

Part of Polishing Your Appearance is understanding how to dress or present yourself for the position or title that you aspire to have. If you want to be a CEO, then dress like one. However, you must understand your body type which gives you the edge when it comes to appearing polished.

Your Body Type

Here are a few items that you should consider when putting your looks together: Your body type is the key component to how your look and style will come across.

Alexander Pezo

Unfortunately, we all are not built like the mannequin in the front window. Make sure that the styles you pick for you compliment your body type.

The three most common fits and body types of men are: Slim, Modern, and Portly
(See Illustration)

Slim Fit clothing refers to any garment that fits the wearer close to the body. For instance. Slim-fit pants have a snug fit through the legs and end in a small leg opening that can be anywhere from 9" to 20" in circumference, depending on size.

Alexander Pezo

Modern Fit refers to up to date cut which is usually related to whatever the current fashion trend is but in moderation. For example, right now the slim fit is the trend. Currently, Modern fit is slim, but not skinny, usually straight through the hips and thighs and with slim line modifications.

Portly Fit is someone that is stocky or overweight. Portly is used as a polite version of overweight. It is for the person who is bulky or mainly oversized from the waist and towards the thighs. They require more room inside their attire and that is exactly what a Portly Suit is designed to accomplish.

In the words of Ralph Waldo Emerson, *"The only person you are destined to become is the person you decide to be."* Knowing who you aspire to be is the first step in the process of learning how to become that individual.

Choosing Your Blazer

Anyone that is preparing to purchase or have a custom blazer made – or simply rent one – must know the three most common collar styles prior to deciding for the occasion's best fit.

Knowing each style will provide you with a better understanding as to which category you fall into. It also provides you with a great idea as to what not to wear.

Now that you have a better understanding of how a suit and your garments should fit, here are the three collar styles and their lapel variations:

Lapels are the folded flaps of cloth on the front of a jacket or coat and are most commonly found on formal clothing and suit jackets. Usually, they are formed by folding over the front edges of the jacket or coat and sewing them to the collar, an extra piece of fabric around the back of the neck.

Alexander Pezo

The Lapel in addition to the cut of the blazer can "Polish Your Appearance" and give your look a whole new dimension. For example, look at actor ***Idris Elba***.

Here are examples of a Notch Lapel, Peak Lapel and Shawl Collar: ***Notch Lapel, David Beckham***

Peak Lapel

Shawl Collar, Dwyane Wade

All blazers either have a center or side vents. *Center Vents* are usually classified as more classy, conservative, corporate, and timeless. *Side Vents* are usually classified as more modern, fashion-forward and contemporary. Here are both options pictured below.

Alexander Pezo

Center Vent

Side vent

"It is hard to move forward if you are constantly looking in the rearview mirror."

Alexander Pezo

The most common color for a suit is blue. Whether for business, formal or a casual blazer, blue is unprecedented, like Former President Barack Obama's everyday look. Blue is one of three primary colors, along with red and green. It's also the most popular color for web design outside of white, and at least 50 additional shades of the color used for web development.

With this stated, if you struggle with making wardrobe and tie decisions in terms of what color to wear for an interview, then choose blue. The color is subtle and will not come across as overbearing to a potential interviewer and will even be deemed as familiar. To most, you will also appear trustworthy and confident. This is a crucial factor when interviewing for jobs where reliability is a prerequisite.

Alexander Pezo

Red ties state that the wearer is assertive and confident. If you are looking to make an instant impression while being interviewed for a job requiring confidence, this piece will seal the deal. According to research, darker colors tend to be positive.

Here is what a few colors may indicate about you and those that choose them:

Alexander Pezo

For those that gravitate toward the color black, it indicates an artsy and sensitive nature; blue leads towards steady, harmony, reliability and empathy; and brown says a sense of dependability and more substance than show. Those who choose white indicate a great deal of logic and order, while those who prefer red are assertive, aggressive and determined with their efforts. With that stated, wearing a combination of black, white and a hint of red could be deemed a winning combination in any boardroom.

The choice of a purple/orange color for a tie is out of the box for a job interview, but that does not mean it's not a positive thing. People who are drawn towards those colors usually enjoy learning and gaining knowledge as well as paying it forward on what they have learned from others. These individuals are outgoing, maybe even a bit eccentric, and someone that others easily gravitate towards.

Alexander Pezo

If you are in the creative industries or are forging a career path or meeting a client whose business is built on creativity and individuality. These color choices state you tend to self-critique positively, and people who gravitate towards these colors are often game changers in leadership, being unafraid of new processes and departmental restructuring.

A splash of purple/orange to refine your business suit, is one way of projecting an appearance that conveys positive energy and thinking outside the box.

Color ultimately, in most cases, define who you are. Michael Schenker once said; *"If everyone would look for that uniqueness, then we would have a very colorful world."*

Alexander Pezo

White Dress Shirt   **White Dress Shirt**

Understanding your end game plays a major role in polishing your appearance.

The Shirt Collar

Wearing the correct shirt collar is a key component when it comes to "Polishing Your Appearance."

Here is a breakdown of the shirt collars that I recommend you wear to compliment your suit:

The Classic Pinpoint which is, as stated, a pointy collar.

The Spread Collar has a wider **collar** which points are angled outwards instead of pointing down. It suits men with slim or long faces, or anyone who appreciates a modern twist to traditional attire. The ***spread collar*** with a full or half Windsor knot, is among easiest tie knots to master.

Tab are when a man's dress **shirt collar** is "tabbed," it has two small **tabs** in the middle of the **collar** points. These connect beneath the necktie, pushing the knot up and out.

Alexander Pezo

The *Cutaway* referred to as the Pat Riley collar is an angled cut away from the center button. Although there is a multitude of additional options for shirts, this should give you a solid starting point. With the right suit, shirt, tie and shoes, at a glance this starts the process of "Polishing Your Appearance." However; remember the primary objective is to enhance your wardrobe while preparing yourself for the next phase of personal growth.

CHAPTER 4

THE POLISHED MENTOR

A Mentor is **an experienced and trusted adviser.** This also means to, "Pay it Forward" to the next generation of young men that may or may not have someone to show them the way. Prior to writing the first chapter or even coming up with the concept, it was important for me to recognize my life's mentors.

Michael Artis, known as A-Frame, from East Chicago played collegiate basketball at the University of Cincinnati. He took a liking to me at a young age. He would come to pick me up as a middle school kid and take me to open gym. Withrow High School at the time had the best open gym on the Eastside of the city, and like "Polishing My Appearance" was important, esthetically, it was even more important as a basketball player aspiring to get a free ride to college.

The most important part of spending time with Coach Artis for me was just picking his brain about his business endeavors. See, he was the first entrepreneur that I had ever come across. An **Entrepreneur** is *a person who organizes and operates a business or businesses, taking on greater than normal financial risks in order to do so.*

This was intriguing to me because, to be honest, he was the first African American male that I had ever met that wanted to do something other than just get a 9 to 5 job. Understand, I am not knocking having a steady job. However; there is a quote that says; *"You can either work for someone else's dreams or you can chase your own."*

They say, "It takes a village to raise a child." The reality of this statement ultimately saved my life. Hopefully as you read this chapter, you realize the importance of having multiple mentors. More importantly, you will understand that paying it forward is how you ultimately receive blessings and God's grace.

The baton was passed on from Mike Artist to Joe Eley. It was without a doubt Joe that took interest in me and started taking me to Xavier basketball games. It was thanks to Joe that I was able to meet the XU Coaching Staff in Bob Staak, Jerry Wainwright Wayne Morgan and Mike Sussli. Thanks to Joe, I was able to get to know players such as Dexter Bailey, Walter McBride, Eddie Johnson, Jeff Jenkins, Leroy Greenidge, Anthony Hicks, Vick Fleming and the school's all-time leading scorer, Byron Larkin.

This was vital to assisting with "Polishing My Appearance" because, again, I was able to see positive images of black males cultivating relationships that would ultimately change their lives. More importantly it continued to build my confidence that I could one day see my way to success. From going to the games, to visiting their dorm rooms, and watching them get interviewed by the local media, I was able to see another way to start "Polishing My Appearance." Being comfortable getting interviewed by the media and understanding how to answer them takes a special kind of Polish. All I can think while writing this part of the book is that; *"Perfect Practice Prevents Poor Performance."*

These experiences, along with going to basketball camps at Western Kentucky whose Assistant Coach was a young Dwayne Casey (now the Detroit Pistons coach) assisted me. Coach Casey showed me at a young age the importance of doing the right thing. As a rising 9th grader, while participating at the Western Kentucky basketball camp, my Wittnauer Watch was stolen. Somehow the word got back to Casey, and he (in private) gave me a $100 bill. I say this not to stir up any controversy over this, but because in my opinion, Dwayne did the right thing. It was less about the NCAA's rules and regulations, and more about helping a young man in a time of distress.

Joe then took me to my first All-American Camp, BC All-Stars in Rensselaer, Indiana. It was due to this opportunity that I was able to get my first letter of interest from NBA Hall of Famer and Creighton University Coach, Willis Reed. Thinking back, the talent on the bus ride to Indiana was unprecedented. Notre Dame shooting sensation, Joe Frederick, long-time NBA Coach Monte Mathis, Counselor and Xavier Guard-Forward, Walter McBride, Withrow point guard, John Thomas, and North College Hill high-riser, Chuck Broadnax.

Joe, without a doubt, is the reason that I was able to get into The Summit Country Day School and go on to become First-Team all-city as a freshman playing varsity basketball.

This book would not be complete or possible without recognizing the contribution that Joe Eley made in my life.

"Joe was an AAU guy before his time and would have been a great grassroots basketball guy long before the terminology was cool."

With all due respect to all of my mentors, my lifetime mentor unequivocally is Fred Geraci.

Alexander Pezo

I met Fred at the age of 15 as a sophomore at Purcell-Marian High School. I still remember to this day the first question he ever asked me in the school cafeteria.

"How are your grades?" Fred asked me.

I quickly replied, "Who mines?"

He replied, "Yes, mine!" Without me even noticing it, he had already started the process of "Polishing My Appearance."

Throughout the year he and I forged a relationship that I am still thankful for to this day. He invited me into his home, introduced me to his wife and kids, but more importantly, he made me feel as if I were a part of his family. The relationship was extremely important to me on multiple fronts. As I mentioned before, growing up without a father in the home led me to seek out males that were doing the things that I eventually wanted to do.

Remember, earlier in the book when Red said, *"Son I cannot afford anything outside of your education. However I can afford to put you in position to meet that kind of people."* So, when the opportunity to have a mentor such as Mr. Geraci came about, it was a blessing that I could not have imagined.

You see, a part of "Polishing Your Appearance" should be to seek out individuals that are living the type of balanced lifestyle that you aspire to have. With that said, Fred Geraci was a Christian, husband, father of four kids, teacher, and fly dresser. More importantly, he was a former collegiate basketball and baseball player. The reason I bring this up is to show why it was easy for him to grab my attention because of his sports background.

When picking a mentor, it is always wise to find someone that you have things in common with. This normally exposes you to a great deal of opportunities that you never imagined. For example, Fred was a well-known tennis pro and repairer of clay and sand courts in and throughout Cincinnati and Northern Kentucky. Again, as a kid that grew up at 3340 Woodburn in the inner-city, this was a great chance for me to experience those situations that "Red" had positioned me to do. In fact, I was "Polishing My Appearance" in a multitude of ways I had no idea about.

Having a mentor like Geraci exposed me to working places where I couldn't afford to venture. It showed me at the ripe age of sixteen that anything is possible with hard work. Also, it did a great deal for my confidence. You will hear more about confidence versus arrogance in the final chapter of the book. To me, the single most important quality to "Polishing Your Appearance" is understanding and being comfortable with who you are. The more that I worked with folks from different cultures at a young age, the better I felt about my appearance and articulating to others.

There is a famous quote from Theodore Roosevelt that says; ***"Each time we face our fear, we gain strength, courage, and confidence in the doing."***

In addition to our sports connection, Geraci was a phenomenal person and unbelievable dresser. His style was subtle and smooth with a classy, smooth flare. As a mentor, he personified, "Modeling the way."

I still remember to this day him going with me to Kenwood Mall to pick up my brand-new altered dress slacks from *Zeidler and Zeidler* Men's clothing store. I learned a great deal about style from watching Geraci. Remember, a Mentor is **an experienced and trusted adviser.** This also means to "Pay it Forward" to the next generation of young men that may or may not have someone to show them the way.

Geraci always seemed to show me the way in a multitude of facets. However, it was emulating his style that grabbed my attention at that point and time. His style in many regards was unprecedented and always a topic of discussion amongst guys such as me and Frank Fields.

According to Frank, in his opinion, ***"Geraci was that smooth, cool teacher who was just a super chill dude that you had the utmost respect for. The way that he commanded his class and presented history was second to none. Over the years, only a handful of teachers have had that type of impact."***

When I think back on the effect that Fred Geraci had and still has on my life today, it reminds me of one of my favorite quotes credited to Oprah Winfrey that says, ***"A mentor is someone who allows you to see the hope inside yourself."***

In other words, for me, Geraci empowered me to do better and to want better for my future.

Let the record reflect I had a great deal of trying times as a student-athlete during this point and time in my life. To have someone that empowered and provided me a sense of confidence was more than I could have asked for.

As I stated at the beginning of this chapter a Mentor is **an experienced and trusted adviser.** This also means to **"Pay it Forward"** to the next generation that may or may not have someone to show them the way.

I would again like to say thanks to all of you that took the time to show me how to become a glimpse of everything you all provided me. Leadership, integrity, character, and more importantly, the will to deal with and overcome adversity are at the core of what you taught me.

Again, as Oprah Winfrey was credited with saying; ***"A mentor is someone who allows you to see the hope inside yourself."***

CHAPTER 5

POLISH YOUR GROOMING

A key essential to "Polishing Your Appearance" is understanding the importance of grooming. **Grooming** *is to prepare or train for a particular purpose or activity.*

This is the most overlooked aspect of a man's appearance. Growing up as a young boy the only thing that I understood about grooming was getting a haircut every couple of weeks. The older and more mature that I became, the more important it became to understand the levels of grooming. Over the next couple of pages, I will discuss some of the vital areas of a man's appearance, esthetically.

When walking into a room always remember what Snoop Dogg says; *"You don't get a second chance to make a first impression."* With that stated, great personal hygiene is important. Although this should be an easy part of the equation, men seem to miss the mark continuously in this regard. Hygiene is a vital part of health, wealth, and leading a successful life. You do not want your peers to "smell you" prior to seeing you.

The image you project should be seen and not heard. As my good friend Ron Harris from East Orange always says; *"Always be more substance than show."* People should be able to look at you and tell that you're accomplished without you having to tell them. From head to toe, your "Polish" should be in sync and compliment each other.

Face Washing & Cleansing

Washing your face twice daily is crucial to having clear and healthy skin. As important as this is never use body soap, or body scrubs on your face. Even though this may appear to be a cheaper more convenient route to take in the shower, body soaps tend to strip the skin of its key and natural moisture potentially irritating the pH balance. Most doctors and dermatologist recommend a face cleanser, specifically, to assist with restoring moisture and normalizing your pH balance. If this is not working then I highly recommend getting a referral to a dermatologist.

In the words of **Howard Murad**; *"Healthy skin is a reflection of overall wellness."*

Shaving daily, and on the weekends, is part of "Polishing Your Appearance."

Keep in mind, a potential employer or significant other wants to see you at your best. As the saying goes; *"Stay ready, so you do not have to get ready."*

Men that tend to have tender or sensitive facial skin may need to allow the face to breath one day a week and bypass shaving.

BRUSHING FLOSSING & MOUTHWASH

While it is great to brush your teeth two or three times daily, the importance of flossing after every brushing is key. Men's health can be directly correlated to the benefits of flossing. This should be a daily personal hygiene routine.

Teeth are an area that men often overlook when it comes to personal care and "Polishing Their Appearance." Brushing, flossing, brushing of the tongue along with flossing and mouthwash, will assist with minimizing bad breath.

If you are someone in the spotlight or media, daily, consider a whitening treatment, but make sure that you have no cavities or fillings that need to be addressed.

It's important to say, mouthwash should be a mandatory part of your oral hygiene routine. This is an area that should be emphasized for both you & your kids. This will assist with reducing plaque as well as the number of bacteria that travels in your mouth. However, remember that mouthwash contains fluoride, which helps fight cavities and potential periodontal disease. Also, mouthwash can get in between your teeth and to places that floss and toothpaste cannot. The condition of our mouth can affect how we project to others as well as the confidence that we have in ourselves. The great Maya Angelou said; *"If you only have one smile in you, give it to the one you love."*

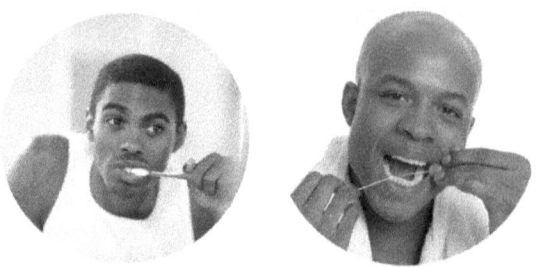

The way I view this quote is that your inner being and presentation in life should bring you more joy than anyone. Be at peace with you always.

Cuticles & Nails

If you think the area of flossing and oral hygiene are a forgotten point of emphasis think again. When you're doing networking events, shaking hands or doing anything where toes are exposed, hygiene is a must.

My Mom always said, *"Pay attention to how a person maintains their hands and feet. It will tell you a great deal about how they maintain the rest of their hygiene."*

Neat and well-maintained nails are high on the list when it comes to attracting a significant other. Therefore, I stay on top of my nails, and highly recommend that other men do so as well.

Having nails that are long enough to collect dirt, have any discoloration or are too long, may require a manicure or pedicure. *Note if you are diabetic or have any other health concerns please consult a physician for proper care.*

Also remember to trim your cuticles, the sides of your nails and use hand and feet moisturizer to keep them soft and prevent calluses and cracking."

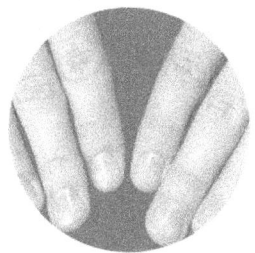

MANSCAPING

Manscaping *is the removal or trimming of hair on a man's body for cosmetic effect.* Every man should become accustomed to doing this. Today, trimming hair everywhere is simply the standard and expectation for a man's hygiene. A good rule of thumb is that if you can twist the hair, then you need to strongly consider shaving or trimming down that area.

Also, there is no reason that any man should allow his nose, ear or stray eyebrow hairs to get out of control. Use this approach when considering how others may look at your nose, ear, and eyebrows. First, you cannot deny that the nose, ear and eyebrow hair exist.

Even if you are at an age where you can no longer maintain these areas yourself, you do not have permission to ignore your nose, ear, and eyebrow hair. Let's be clear, you need to have hair in both places, but it should not be visible to others. Here is a good rule of thumb from the outside looking in: If you are tall, make sure you maintain your nose hair. If you are short, your hair inside your ears and on your lobes should be a major focal point of emphasis. However; if you are serious about "Polishing Your Appearance," I say play it safe and keep both areas clear. Keep in mind if you see them, so do they. If you notice your hairs are sticking out of your nose or ears, those around you do as well. Having a pair of grooming scissors and or a grooming kit are must-haves on every man's gift list.

I will leave you with a profound quote to close this chapter. *"You are your greatest asset. Put your time, effort and money into training, grooming, and encouraging your greatest asset."* **Tom Hopkins**

CHAPTER 6

ARROGANT & CONFIDENT APPEARANCE

There has always been a fine line when it comes to the meaning and perception of arrogance versus confidence. Throughout the journey of "Polishing Your Appearance," you will need a good deal of arrogance and confidence. In life, you will have some peaks and valleys that will require you to believe in you when no one else does.

Arrogance is *having or revealing an exaggerated sense of one's own importance or abilities* while **Confidence** is *a feeling of self-assurance arising from appreciation of one's own abilities or qualities.* Depending upon whom you ask, you will get a plethora of answers to the meaning of both.

The significance of this book having six chapters speaks to every man's imperfections with his work. The number six implies and speaks to a man's imperfection. Thus, in spiritual terms the number six is related to the man and his shortcomings.

In knowing this, we must understand that we will continually encounter situations that calls our confidence into question. Whether it be not getting a job offer, promotion, part in a movie, or opportunity that you felt you deserve, your confidence is what will see you through a ton of heartbreaking moments. Although persistence plays a role, you will not be able to move forward without the belief in oneself.

In chapter 2, I wrote: *"The individual should always make the suit and the suit should not make them."*

Often, on the exterior we look great, but we are broken on the inside. Understand our true appearance is shaped and formed from the inside out. With that said, the purpose for making such a statement is so that everyone understands that without confidence and presence, a suit nor anything about the individual holds any merit. For the record, my confidence has afforded me opportunities that I may not been prepared for at the time. However, my approach and belief in myself allowed me to project that on to the decision maker. Confidence will keep you in the game, so to speak, and arrogance has a way of making you numb to what others may think about your game.

The great Oscar Wilde once said, *"There is only one thing in the world worse than being talked about, and that is not being talked about."* Just remember that.

Success will set you apart from most of your counterparts, unlike anything that you could imagine. Know that it is okay to be "different." We are not all made to "fit in."

Ask yourself this. Do you think *Mahatma Gandhi, Nelson Mandela, Barack Obama, Steve Jobs, and Mark Zuckerberg were concerned about fitting into a box or standing out in the crowd?*

Alexander Pezo

Mohandas Karamchand Gandhi was an Indian activist who was the leader of the Indian independence movement against British rule. Employing nonviolent civil disobedience, Gandhi led India to independence and inspired movements for civil rights and freedom across the world. The honorific Mahātmā – applied to him first in 1914 in South Africa – is now used worldwide. In India, he is also called Bapu and Gandhi ji, and known as the Father of the Nation.

Alexander Pezo

Nelson Rolihlahla Mandela was a South African anti-apartheid revolutionary, political leader, and philanthropist who served as President of South Africa from 1994 to 1999. He was the country's Black head of state and the first elected in a fully representative democratic election. His government focused on dismantling the legacy of apartheid by tackling institutionalized racism and fostering racial reconciliation. Ideologically, an African nationalist and socialist, he served as President of the African National Congress party from 1991 to 1997.

Alexander Pezo

Barack Hussein Obama II is an American attorney and politician who served as the 44th president of the United States from 2009 to 2017. A member of the Democratic Party, he was the first African American to be elected to the presidency. He previously served as a United States senator from Illinois.

Alexander Pezo

Steven Paul Jobs was an American business magnate and investor. He was the chairman, chief executive officer, and co-founder of Apple Inc.; chairman and majority shareholder of Pixar; a member of The Walt Disney Company's board of directors following its acquisition of Pixar; and the founder, chairman, and CEO of NEXT. Jobs is widely recognized as a pioneer of the microcomputer revolution of the 1970s and 1980s, along with Apple co-founder Steve Wozniak.

Mark Elliot Zuckerberg is an American technology entrepreneur and philanthropist. He is known for co-founding and leading Facebook as its chairman and chief executive officer.

Each of these pioneers and trailblazers are wired differently than practically anyone you may know personally. They are great examples of how an individual with arrogance and confidence can affect change in the world. Each was told at some point that their dreams and goals may be far-fetched which affected their confidence. However, their arrogance gave them the will and determination to persevere.

When it comes to you having a balance between arrogance and confidence, never apologize for being you. Just be sure to stay humble and hungry in order to be received in a manner which you desire. Remember, your goal should always be to stay focused on your "end game." It is next to impossible to do so if your character is not polished. **The End Game** *is part of the final process that should be completed to reach your target.*

Alexander Pezo

Remember the words of Ermias Asghedom, AKA Nipsey Hussle who said, "My thing is that I don't give no person that much power over my path that I'm walking. Not one person can make or break what I'm doing, except me or God."

August 15, 1985- March 31, 2019

Whenever you feel yourself falling off track, attempt to reflect on the fact that "Polishing Your Appearance" is more than a state of mind. Also understand you may take some steps backwards prior to moving forward, but ultimately, you can achieve any goal placed in front of you with the understanding that perseverance will eventually overcome imperfections.

Alexander Pezo

ABOUT THE AUTHOR

Born Alexander Mays, "Alexander Pezo" started out as a notable high fashion designer for men & women. However; his business savvy and a love for people and task management, allowed him to expand the brand beyond clothing. Now, Alexander is a blossoming Entrepreneur, Celebrated Sales & Operations Strategist, Renowned Speaker, and Best-Selling Author.

Alexander has spent more than 25 years in Sales & Operations to date in the Staffing Industry is considered an Operations & Team Building Guru. He is the author of two personal image & self-development books, *Polish Your Appearance* and *A Gentleman's Guide to Style & Image*, as well as He is also the author of , *Polish Your Appearance a 30-Day Devotional* & founder of a personal, business, image, wellness & growth community POLISH YOUR APPEARANCE ACADEME.

Alexander has always been very intentional when setting targets for himself. He knew one day that he would run a servant leadership platform while using his gift to tap into individual's & organizations areas for growth. Through POLISH YOUR APPEARANCE ACADEME Alexander will develop individuals, organizations & The Community build their H.O.M.E. (Health, Optimism, Morals, & Evolvement).

Alexander Pezo

"As a unit, we will continue to encourage the heart, hold one another accountable and set actionable targets that are essential to our growth. Developing your core will lend to enhancing your quality of life. We will help you manifest greatness in target areas you have never experienced before. Your Energy Is Key." ~ AP

Alexander earned his master's in athletic administration from one of the country's most renown colleges, Ohio University. Alexander earned his B.A. Degree in English-Journalism from Tennessee Tech University. He was also a two-year letterman on the Golden Eagle Men's Basketball Team. With that said, he is an industry savvy, self-starter, with a knack for Sales & Operations, galvanizing teams, organizations & encouraging the hearts while empowering everyone that he crosses paths with. Alexander's leadership ability has afforded him the opportunity of serving major clients such as BETHer, Friar's Club, YMCA of Atlanta, Love Freedom Movement, Harlem Arts Foundation, Goodwill of Atlanta, Adversity University & PeopleReady. From the playground courts, to image consulting, to the boardroom, the one constant is that Alexander has convincingly excelled at every level. He is bound and determined to maximize his performance by leading from an organic space of practical experience . His skillset and niche are truly a gift.

Originally from Cincinnati, OH, Alexander now lives in Atlanta with his wife and kids. The blend of his two companies, POLISH YOUR APPEARANCE ACADEME & ALEXANDER PEZO are an ideal solution for individuals and organizations seeking leadership development, corporate and cultural.

Alexander Pezo

Alexander is also featured on the cover of black business of Atlanta magazine. He just received the prestigious proclamation from the city of Atlanta deeming December 8th hereunto Alexander Pezo Day.

www.ingramcontent.com/pod-product-compliance
Lightning Source LLC
Chambersburg PA
CBHW070107100426
42743CB00012B/2680